—★ HOME EDITION ★—

GOSPEL PROJECT

FOR KIDS

The Gospel Project: Home Edition
Grades 3-5 Workbook Semester 1

D1518636

Workbook Pages to Supplement
The Gospel Project: Home Edition Teacher's Guide Semester 1

LifeWay Press©,
One LifeWay Plaza, Nashville, TN
37234-0172.
ISBN: 9781535909402
Item 005804774
Dewey Decimal Classification Number: 220.07
Subject Heading: BIBLE—STUDY\THEOLOGY—STUDY\GOSPEL—STUDY

Printed in the United States of America
Kids Ministry Publishing
LifeWay Resources
One LifeWay Plaza
Nashville, TN 37234
Nashville, Tennessee 37234-0172

We believe that the Bible has God for its author; salvation for its end; and truth, without any mixture of error, for its matter and that all Scripture is totally true and trustworthy. To review LifeWay's doctrinal guidelines, please visit *www.lifeway.com/doctrinalguideline*. All Scripture quotations are taken from the Christian Standard Bible © Copyright 2017 by Holman Bible Publishers. Used by permission.

CONTENTS

HOW TO USE THIS BOOK

For Kids

Congratulations! You are about to take an 18-week journey through the beginning of the story of the Bible, from Creation through Moses.

You are going to learn that although the Bible has a lot of stories, there is really one big story that is being told of God's plan for people. It shows God's great salvation plan: God created us. We sinned. God promised us a Savior and sent Him—Jesus—for us. Jesus died for us so we might live with God forever. We respond by believing. (See page 62.)

For Parents

Use these activity pages, Bible stories, and teaching pictures as directed during the 18 weeks of teaching plans in *The Gospel Project: Home Edition Teacher Guide Semester 1* (005793045) or *The Gospel Project: Home Edition Digital Teacher Guide Semester 1* (005804814).

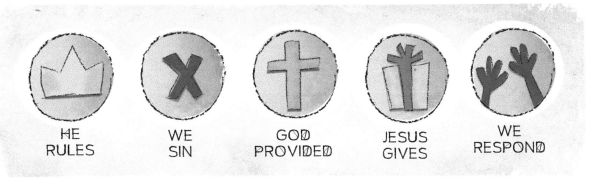

HE RULES   WE SIN   GOD PROVIDED   JESUS GIVES   WE RESPOND

Did you notice that you are part of God's plan? Yes, it's true! Jesus died for you, and you can respond and believe to become part of God's ongoing plan to bring others to know Him. Let's take this journey together!

THE BIG QUESTION

Why did God create the world?
Unscramble the words to find the answer.

GOD ⦿⦿⦿⦿⦿⦿⦿
ACDTREE

THE ⦿⦿⦿⦿⦿ AND
WODLR

⦿⦿⦿⦿⦿⦿⦿⦿⦿⦿
TERNVIYGEH

IN IT FOR HIS ⦿⦿⦿⦿⦿
RGLOY

Creation Scene Search

Two of these animals are NOT in the creation scene.
Can you find them?

What part of God's creation do you enjoy the most? Describe it here or draw a picture of something God created.

the pikser is thees and animls

FAMILY DISCUSSION STARTERS
Discuss with your family or journal your answers.

- What are some things God created? (See Genesis 1–2.)

- What does it mean to bring God glory? (*We can show people how awesome God is.*)

- How can you and your family bring God glory this week?

DAY SIX CROSSWORD

Use the clues to solve the crossword puzzle.

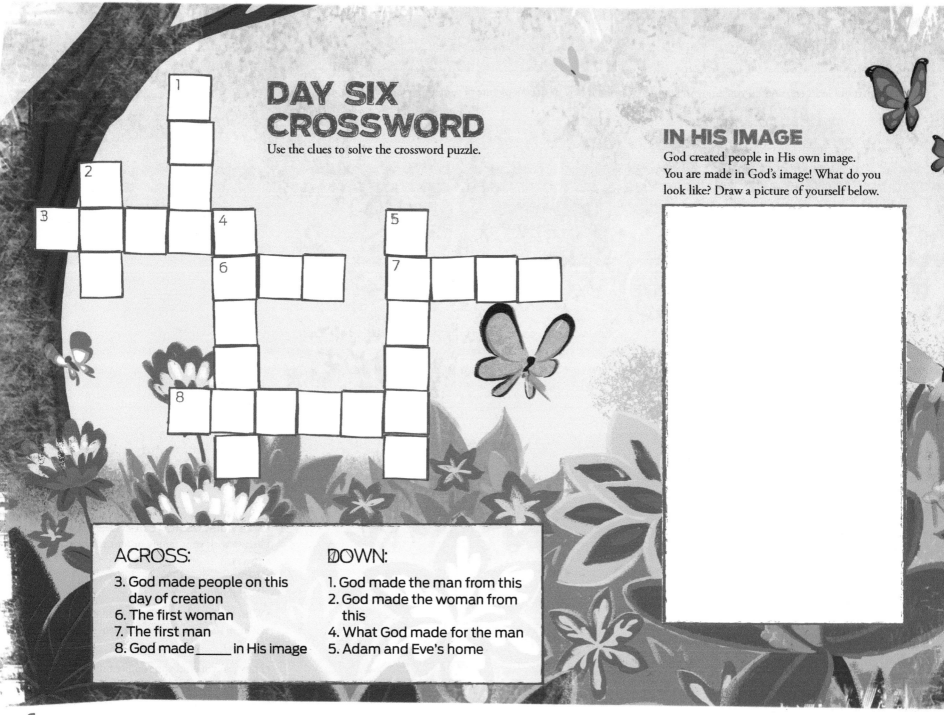

IN HIS IMAGE

God created people in His own image. You are made in God's image! What do you look like? Draw a picture of yourself below.

ACROSS:

3. God made people on this day of creation
6. The first woman
7. The first man
8. God made _____ in His image

DOWN:

1. God made the man from this
2. God made the woman from this
4. What God made for the man
5. Adam and Eve's home

Journal Page

God created the world and everything in it for His glory. List ways you could use your unique characteristics to bring God glory. Or write a short prayer, thanking God for creating you in His own image.

FAMILY DISCUSSION STARTERS

Discuss with your family or journal your answers.

• How did God create Adam and Eve? (See Genesis 1:26–2:25.)

• What does it mean to be created in God's image? (*We have qualities similar to God like being wise, loving, and creative; but we are not God. He is all-knowing, ever compassionate, and the Creator.*)

• How can you and your family recognize God's image in each other this week?

OUT OF EDEN

WHEN ADAM AND EVE SINNED, GOD SENT THEM OUT OF THE GARDEN OF EDEN. START IN THE CENTER OF THE MAZE AND WORK YOUR WAY OUT.

START

WHAT IS SIN?

Cross out every third letter. Write the remaining letters in the blanks below to find the answer.

S	I	R	N	I
K	S	B	W	R
E	C	A	K	K
I	N	V	G	G
N	O	D	M	S
L	T	A	W	E

SIN IS BREAKING GOD'S LAW

8

SIN ENTERED THE WORLD

Think of a time you did something wrong. What was your punishment? Write about or draw a picture of how you felt. The Bible says we deserve to die for our sin, but Jesus came to rescue us from sin. How does this good news make you feel?

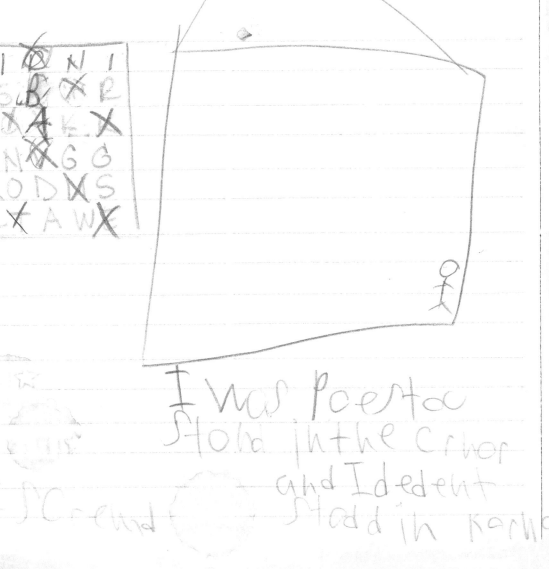

I was poesto Stold in the crnor and I dedent Stadd in Karnor

FAMILY DISCUSSION STARTERS
Discuss with your family or journal your answers.
- What were the consequences of Adam and Eve's sin? (See Genesis 3:16-19.)
- What are some ways that you have sinned?
- How does Jesus help us with our sin problem? (*Jesus paid for sin on the cross so everyone who trusts Him is forgiven. He also frees us from sin. The Holy Spirit helps us resist temptation.*)

KEY WORD SEARCH

Find the key words from the Bible story. Words may appear horizontally, vertically, or diagonally.

- CAIN
- ADAM
- EVE
- SETH
- FLOCK
- ABEL
- SHEPHERD
- SONS
- FIELD
- SIN
- OFFERING
- PUNISHMENT

```
Q A G M S I N Y Q L Z L
H R K G Y W S O N S D K
C A I N J R J D J R G L
K P U N I S H M E N T Z
K J B Z L K M H I L U I
K P O J C S P R S E Z Z
H F Y O V E E M W B V Y
L Q L K H F I T D G O E
W F O S F G M L H A X W
K W A O C A E T S D A U
E B X D D I O Y A B E L
R X X A F A M W R S L X
```

CAIN'S CODE

Fill in the names of the Bible books to decode the secret message.

GENESIS
EXODUS
LEVITICUS
NUMBERS
DEUTERONOMY
JOSHUA

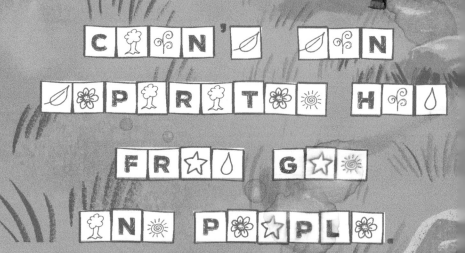

C A N ' S   A N
S P I R I T S   H O
F R O G   G O S
N O   P E O P L E .

Journal Page

Sin not only hurts your relationship with God, it hurts your relationships with others. Can you think of someone who might feel hurt by something you did? Write his or her name below. This week, ask that person for forgiveness.

FAMILY DISCUSSION STARTERS

Discuss with your family or journal your answers.

- What offering did Cain and Abel bring? (See Genesis 4:3-4.)

- Cain sinned. What is the required punishment for sin? (See Romans 3:23; 6:23.)

- How can your family bring an offering to God this week?

NOAH'S MAZE

Make your way through the maze. Collect the letters along the correct path to discover the secret word.

_ _ _ _ _ _ _

START →

FINISH

THE GREAT RESCUE

Use the key to decode the question.
Then write the answer in the blank.

WH_   _ _ _ K   _H_
  15   20 15 15   20   5

P_ _ _ SHM _ _ _
 21 14 9   5 14 20

F_R   _ _R   S_ _?
15   15 21   9 14

_____

1=A	2=B	3=C	4=D	5=E	6=F
7=G	8=H	9=I	10=J	11=K	12=L
13=M	14=N	15=O	16=P	17=Q	18=R
19=S	20=T	21=U	22=V	23=W	26=Z

Journal Page

God put a rainbow in the sky to remind Noah and his descendants of His promise. Use crayons or markers to write the words of Genesis 9:11 below. The flood did not take away sin. When you see a rainbow, remember the story of Noah and that God sent His Son, Jesus, to rescue people from sin.

FAMILY DISCUSSION STARTERS

Discuss with your family or journal your answers.

- Why did God send a flood? (*to punish the world for sin*)

- What punishment do we deserve for our sin? (See Romans 6:23.)

- How does God rescue us from our sin?

WORLD LANGUAGES

Can you guess the official languages of these countries? Write the language below the country's name.

(Languages: Arabic, English, French, Mandarin Chinese, Spanish)

CHINA
_____

SPAIN
_____

SAUDI ARABIA
_____

CAMEROON
_____

Main Point Mix-Up

These words are all mixed up! Can you make sense of them? (Hint: The first letters are in the correct positions.)

SOUTH AFRICA
_____

GDO CEDARET
POLEEP TO
GEVI GROYL
TO HMI AEONL.

Journal Page

Write a prayer of thanks and recognition to God, giving Him glory. God created people to give glory to Him alone. We give God glory when we show or tell about how great He is. God deserves our worship. He is so good!

FAMILY DISCUSSION STARTERS

Discuss with your family or journal your answers.

- Who mattered more to the people—themselves or God?

- How have you been tempted to use your talents to make people think you are great?

- How can you use your talents to show how great God is?

COUNT the STARS

Can you count all the stars on this page? How many did you find? _____

CONSTELLATION SEARCH

Search for the 4-pointed stars. Color them in to reveal a special word.

God made a covenant to

___ ___ ___ ___ ___

His people. God sent Jesus to be born on earth into Abraham's family. Through Jesus, all the nations of the earth are blessed.

Journal Page

Make a list of blessings—things for which you are thankful. Every good gift comes from God. (See James 1:17.)

FAMILY DISCUSSION STARTERS
Discuss with your family or journal your answers.
- What promises have you made? Did you keep them? Why or why not?
- Abraham had faith in God's promise. What is faith? (See Hebrews 11:1.)
- How has Jesus blessed your family?

WHAT'S WRONG?

Some of the things in this scene are wrong.
Find and circle the six items that do not belong.

GOD PROVIDED

Use the code to color the picture. What did God provide
as a sacrifice for Isaac? Whom did God provide as a
sacrifice for us?

1-Brown 2-Yellow 3-Black 4- Green

Journal Page

Write about a tough situation you currently face or a question you have about the future. Pray about those things this week and ask God to help you trust Him and His plan.

FAMILY DISCUSSION STARTERS
Discuss with your family or journal your answers.
- Sometimes it is hard to obey. Tell about a time when obeying was hard for you.
- Whom did God provide as our substitute? (*Jesus took the punishment we deserve for our sin.*)

Jacob's Poem

Use the words below to complete the poem.
Each word can be used only once.

WORD BANK

covenant   Isaac
Esau   prayed
family   promise
God   stone

A Great Promise

Look up the verses to fill in the missing names.
Then use the code to discover the message.
Hint: 3-4 means third name, fourth letter.

God gave His promise to

1. ___ B ___ A ___ A ___ (Genesis 25:5)

2. ___ ___ A ___ C (Genesis 25:20)

3. JAC ___ B (Genesis 28:10)

G ___ D   ___ L W ___ Y ___
  3-4   2-4   1-1   2-2

K E E P ___   ___ ___ ___
      2-2   1-5 2-1 2-2

P ___ ___ ___ ___ ___ E ___
1-3 3-4 1-7 2-1 2-2   2-2

Long, long ago, a _____ was made.
God said to Abram, "I heard when you _____.
I'm making a _____ between you and Me.
You'll have blessings and land and a
   big _____."

God kept His promise; He gave Abraham a son.
The son's name was _____, but God was
   not done.
When Isaac grew up, he was Daddy to two,
But Jacob tricked _____ and gave him
   some stew.

Jacob got scared and ran far from home.
He slept on the ground, his pillow a _____.
Then _____ spoke to Jacob so Jacob
   would know, "I'll always be with you,
   wherever you go."

Are any other members of your family believers? Are your parents or grandparents? List their names or draw their pictures. This week, pray for the members of your family.

FAMILY DISCUSSION STARTERS

Discuss with your family or journal your answers.

- God's promise to Abraham was also for whom? (*all of Abraham's future family*)

- What did Jacob see in his dream? (See Genesis 28:12.)

- How can a person get to heaven?

Code Words

Use the code to figure out the name below. Then try using the code to write your own name!

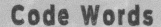

a b c d e f g h i
j k l m n o p q r
s t u v w x x y z

__ __ __ __ __

_____

Your Name

Jacob or Esau?

Do you remember the facts about these brothers? Circle the letter beneath the person described by each statement. Then write the circled letters in the blanks.

	Jacob	Esau
1. He was a hunter.	C	B
2. He worked at home.	L	H
3. He was the younger brother.	E	O
4. He was the older brother.	T	S
5. Isaac favored him.	M	S
6. Rebekah favored him.	I	E
7. He was hairy.	J	N
8. He tricked his father.	G	A

Jacob stole Esau's

__ __ __ __ __ __ __ __ .

Journal Page

List plans you have for the upcoming week or plans you have for the future. Remember, nothing can stop God's perfect plan.

FAMILY DISCUSSION STARTERS
Discuss with your family or journal your answers.
- Which son did God say would serve the other? (See Genesis 25:23.)
- How did God make His plan happen? (*Esau gave his birthright to Jacob.*)
- Is it ever OK to lie or to trick someone? (*No, sin is never OK.*)

WHAT CAN STOP GOD'S PLAN?

Use the big picture answer to find your way through the puzzle, one letter at a time.

START

```
N  O  T  H  S  C  A
E  D  O  I  N  G  N
K  S  G  P  O  T  S
C  P  E  R  M  H  O
      F  E  C  K
      A  P  T  E
      Y  L  A  N
            END
```

NAME CHANGERS

God changed Jacob's name! Write the first letter of each picture to discover Jacob's new name. We've done the first one for you.

I

_____

_____

_____

_____

_____

Journal Page

List things about yourself that make you unique. What makes you different from your friends or siblings? Your interests or hobbies or likes and dislikes might help describe you, but if you are a believer, your true identity is "child of God."

FAMILY DISCUSSION STARTERS

Discuss with your family or journal your answers.

• Tell about a time you were afraid. What did you do?

• What was Jacob's new name? (See Genesis 32:28.)

• Have you ever been forgiven? How did you feel?

SENT AWAY

Can you discover where Joseph was sent? For each letter, go forward two letters in the alphabet. Then write the letters in the blanks.

C E W N R

Evil for Good

Unscramble the words to discover the main poin[t]

ODG _____   SEDU _____

EP'SOJSH _____   FRESUFNG _____

ROF _____   ODGO _____

JOSEPH SENT TO EGYPT

Journal Page

Draw a picture of Joseph when he first arrived in Egypt and a picture of Joseph after he was given a position of power in Egypt. God was with Joseph in Egypt. When we suffer or when others suffer, we can trust that God is in control of all things. He is good.

FAMILY DISCUSSION STARTERS

Discuss with your family or journal your answers.

- Why did Joseph's brothers hate Joseph?

- Have you ever felt envious, wanting what someone else had?

- How is Jesus like Joseph? (*Both of them were betrayed by people close to them.*)

Can You Recognize It?

Circle where each of these close-ups appear in the picture.

Path to Egypt

Words in maze: sent, establish, Joseph, Egypt, establish, Egypt, to, a, God, Joseph, to, remnant, sent, God, a

Journal Page

Think about who is in control of everything. Write about something you worry about. Can God take care of that? Can God make good come of it? God does everything for His glory and our good.

FAMILY DISCUSSION STARTERS
Discuss with your family or journal your answers.

• How did Joseph's dreams come true?

• How did God use evil for good?

• When someone wrongs you, do you choose to forgive or to seek revenge?

Hidden on the Nile

Use the code to determine the color of each space. The final picture will be revealed as each shape is filled.

- 1= Gray
- 2= Light Brown
- 3= Brown
- 4= Black
- 5= Red
- 6= Light Blue

Truth Translation

Can you figure out the message? Fill in the blanks by matching each symbol to the letter in the key.

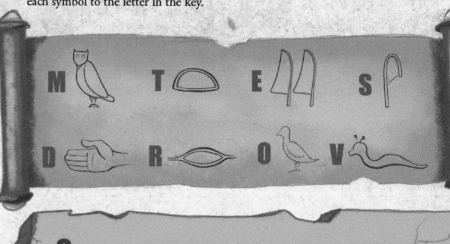

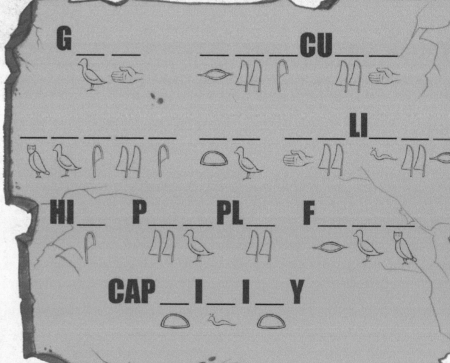

G _ _ _   _ _ _ _ CU _ _ _

_ _ _ _ _ _ _ _ _ _ _ _ _ LI _ _ _ _

HI _ _ P _ _ PL _ _ F _ _ _ _ _

CAP _ _ I _ I _ Y

Journal Page

Write about a time you did something great such as earning a good grade or scoring a goal in a big game. Then write a sentence or two prayer, giving God glory for your accomplishments.

FAMILY DISCUSSION STARTERS

Discuss with your family or journal your answers.

• What name did God use to identify Himself to Moses? (See Exodus 3:13-14.)

• The story of Moses points to whose greater calling and rescue? (*the call of Jesus to come to earth to save people from sin*)

• How can God use you? How can you give Him the credit?

The Plagues Sudoku

Fill in the boxes using the pictures: frog, fly, cow, hail, locust, or darkness. Every row and column and every group of 6 boxes inside the thicker lines must contain each picture only once.

God's Plan for Rescue

Can you remember the 10 plagues? Fill in the plagues. Then use the circled letters to complete the special message.

(Tip: Look up the Scripture reference in the Bible if you need help!)

BL(1)OD   B(7)ILS

F(2)O(3)S   HAIL

G(4)ATS   LOC(8)STS

FLI(5)S   DARKN(9)SS

LIVES(6)OCK   (10)EATH

God proved to the Egyptians that He is the

___ ___ ___   ___ ___ ___ ___   ___ ___ ___
1 4 5   6 2 8 9   3 7 10

Imagine how the Israelites felt during the plagues. How did the Egyptians probably feel? Write a few sentences describing what you know about God. How do you know that He is the one true God?

FAMILY DISCUSSION STARTERS
Discuss with your family or journal your answers.

- How did God prove His power to the Egyptians?

- What animal did the Israelites kill at Passover? (*a lamb*)

- Who is known as the Lamb of God? (See John 1:29.)

- Do you trust God? Why or why not?

Search for Water

Help Moses lead the Israelites through the wilderness to find food and water. Collect the letters along the way to discover a special truth about God.

START

FINISH

Food for Life

Cross out every third letter from left to right, starting at the top row and working down. Fill in the blanks to reveal the answer to the question, Who does Jesus say He is? Then read John 6:31-35 in the Bible.

Jesus is ___ ___ ___ ___ ___ ___ ___ ___

___ ___ ___ ___ ___ ___. (John 6:31-35)

T	H	C	E	B
S	R	E	Q	A
D	M	O	F	T
L	I	H	F	E

Journal Page

Write a short prayer thanking God for providing for you or your family in a time of need.

FAMILY DISCUSSION STARTERS
Discuss with your family or journal your answers.
- Why did the Israelites complain in the wilderness?
- How did God provide for the Israelites?
- List your family's needs. Then pray and ask God to provide.

Golden Calves

Can you find all 20 golden calves
hidden in this picture? Circle each one.

A Closer Look

Take a closer look at the picture. Find the 9 hidden words and
unscramble them to write out the main point of today's Bible story.

_____ _____ _____ _____ _____ _____

_____ _____ _____

Journal Page

God sent His Son, Jesus, to rescue us from sin. When we trust in Him, our sins are forgiven! Write a few sentences about how this good news makes you feel.

FAMILY DISCUSSION STARTERS

Discuss with your family or journal your answers.

• Why did Aaron make a golden calf?

• Moses talked to God for the Israelites. Who talks to God for us?

• An *idol* is anything a person puts in the place of God. What things might be idols in your life?

A Perfect Copy

Draw the picture in the space provided. How close can you get to a perfect copy?

Exodus 20 Picture Puzzle

Try to solve this picture puzzle. What are the letters and pictures saying?

-T + -PUTER + + -OG +

THE TEN COMMANDMENTS: LOVE GOD

Journal Page

List or draw pictures of things you are very good at doing. Circle anything you are perfect at doing. Consider this: Is anyone is perfect at keeping God's laws?

FAMILY DISCUSSION STARTERS

Discuss with your family or journal your answers.

- What does it mean that God is holy?

- List the Ten Commandments.

- What rules does your family have? Why does your family have rules?

Set Apart

Most of these items have a match. Find and circle the object that does not have a match.

What's the Point?

Number the words or phrases to put today's main point in the correct order. Then write the main point in the space provided.

Him	help us know	God gave
us rules to	how to love	and others

_____

_____

_____

Journal Page

Write down one of the Ten Commandments you have trouble obeying. Jesus obeyed the law perfectly for us. God does not accept us because we obey Him; He accepts us because we trust in Jesus.

FAMILY DISCUSSION STARTERS

Discuss with your family or journal your answers.

• Why did God give us rules?

• Which rules are hardest for you to follow? Why?

• Does God accept us based on our ability to obey His commands?

Tools for the Tabernacle

Unscramble the names of the supplies needed to build the tabernacle. If you need help, find and read the verses in your Bible.

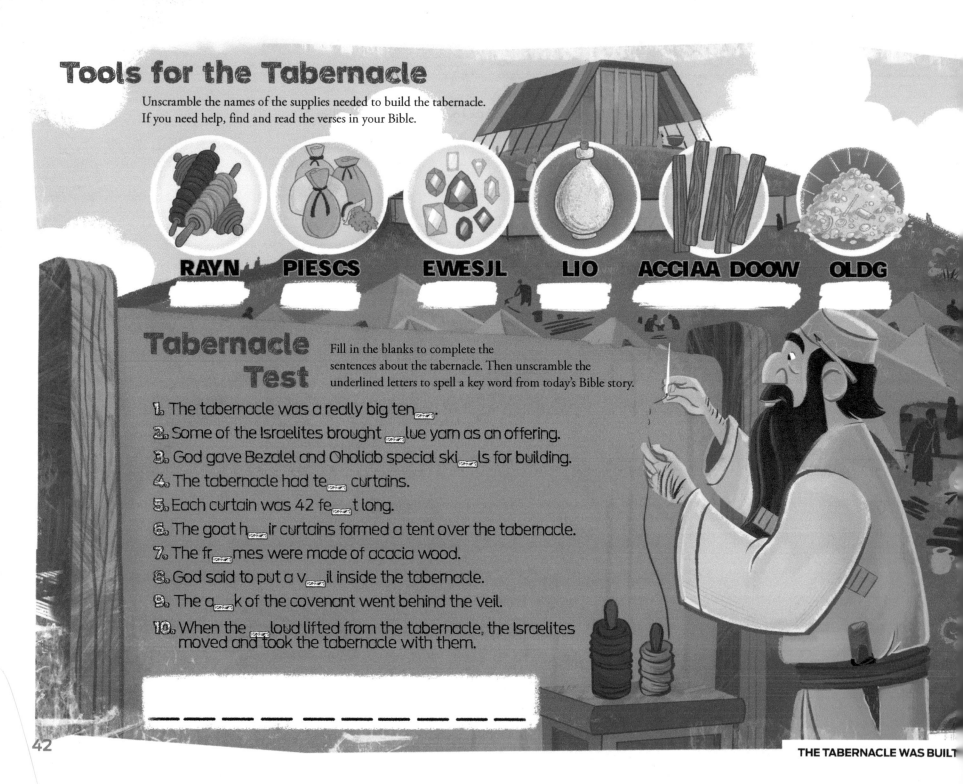

RAYN

PIESCS

EWESJL

LIO

ACCIAA DOOW

OLDG

Tabernacle Test

Fill in the blanks to complete the sentences about the tabernacle. Then unscramble the underlined letters to spell a key word from today's Bible story.

1. The tabernacle was a really big ten___.
2. Some of the Israelites brought ___lue yarn as an offering.
3. God gave Bezalel and Oholiab special ski___ls for building.
4. The tabernacle had te___ curtains.
5. Each curtain was 42 fe___t long.
6. The goat h___ir curtains formed a tent over the tabernacle.
7. The fr___mes were made of acacia wood.
8. God said to put a v___il inside the tabernacle.
9. The a___k of the covenant went behind the veil.
10. When the ___loud lifted from the tabernacle, the Israelites moved and took the tabernacle with them.

_____ _____ _____ _____ _____

42

Journal Page

Write a few sentences describing how you feel knowing that Jesus brings people back to God. Through Jesus, believers are no longer separated from Him!

FAMILY DISCUSSION STARTERS

Discuss with your family or journal your answers.

- What was the purpose of the tabernacle?
- Who brings sinners back to God?
- How can your family spend time with God?

That's Not Right!

Some things in this picture are not right at all! Circle the things that are out of place.

```
O P Z N A I I Z U W Y K U S A
S A C R I F I C E O R G C E T
F I E Z S S T H F Y L O H T O
B I W V Y N K F P P E R O I N
F J U J R W E L U R W B S L E
B Q C U G R P O R R E N A E M
B C B L I W J A E Y J P G A E
T S T N E M D N A M M O C R N
K U G S L A M I N A Y D E S T
Z B Z K J A N R U L E S S I I
```

Search and Sacrifices

Can you find all of the words in the word search? Find and circle in the puzzle each word from the word list.

ANIMALS	CLEAN	COMMANDMENTS
ATONEMENT	SACRIFICE	JEWELRY
PURE	SIN	BURNT
HOLY	OBEY	RULES
ISRAELITES	OFFERING	

Journal Page

Write Romans 12:1 below. A *living sacrifice* means living in a way that pleases God. What are some ways you can worship God with your actions or attitude?

FAMILY DISCUSSION STARTERS
Discuss with your family or journal your answers.
- How did people in the Old Testament pay for sin?
- Why don't we offer sacrifices to pay for our sin? Who can take away our sin?
- Write a thank-you prayer to Jesus for being the ultimate sacrifice for sin.

Who Else?

Trace the main point of today's Bible story. Put your pencil in the start space and follow these directions. Write down each letter you pass over.

Move...
1. up 2 spaces
2. right 1 space
3. down 5 spaces
4. right 2 spaces
5. up 2 spaces
6. right 4 spaces
7. up 1 space
8. left 5 spaces
9. up 2 spaces
10. right 6 spaces
11. down 5 spaces
12. left 4 spaces
13. up 1 space

E	L	N	O	O	T	H	E	R
H	O	S	G	E	R	S	H	B
T	R	I	E	R	E	H	T	E
E	D	T	I	S	G	O	D	S
G	A	S	E	M	B	L	R	I
T	L	O	N	I	H	S	E	D

Start

___ ___ ___   ___ ___ ___ ___

___ ___ ___ ___ ___ ___ ___

___ ___ ___ ___ ___ ___ ___ ___ ___

___ ___ ___ ___ ___ ___

___ ___ ___ ___ ___ ___ ___ ___

___ ___ ___ ___ ___ ___ ___ ___

___ ___ ___

Commandment Confusion

Read these commandments. Some of them do not belong. Cross out any commands that are not part of the Ten Commandments. (See Exodus 20:1-17.)

1. Do no have other gods besides the one true God.

2. Brush and floss twice daily.

3. Do not misuse the name of the Lord.

4. Look both ways before crossing the street.

5. Honor your father and mother, if you like what they say.

6. Get 10 hours of sleep every night.

7. Do not kill.

8. Do not steal.

9. Lie when it keeps you out of trouble.

10. Do not want what belongs to someone else.

Challenge: Which of the Ten Commandments are missing from this list?

Journal Page

List two or three things you remember about today's Bible story. Also write something you can do this week to show God that you love Him.

FAMILY DISCUSSION STARTERS
Discuss with your family or journal your answers.
- What did Moses say about remembering God's commands? (See Deuteronomy 4:40.)

- Who is like God?

- How can you show God that you love Him?

Repeat These Things

Read Deuteronomy 6:7 in your Bible. Can you find in this scene the four scenarios described in the verse? Circle each one.

A Crossword to Remember

God reminded His people of His covenant with them. Solve this crossword to see how much you remember from the Bible story.

DOWN
1. where the Israelites wandered for 40 years
2. the promised land
3. rules and laws God gave to show us how to love God and others
4. the man who led God's people out of Egypt
6. the one who would lead God's people into the promised land

ACROSS
5. an agreement
7. where God gave Moses the Ten Commandments
8. God's people, a stubborn people
9. where the Israelites were slaves

WORD BOX

COVENANT,
MOUNT SINAI,
CANAAN, EGYPT,
ISRAELITES,
COMMANDMENTS,
WILDERNESS,
MOSES, JOSHUA

48

Journal Page

Memorizing Scripture helps us remember who God is and what He has done. Write out the key passage or another verse you want to memorize this week.

FAMILY DISCUSSION STARTERS
Discuss with your family or journal your answers.

- What did God want His people to remember?

- Tell about a Bible story you heard recently. What do you remember?

- Choose a verse or passage of Scripture for your family to memorize this week.

God Created the World
Genesis 1:1-25

MAIN POINT: GOD CREATED EVERYTHING FOR HIS GLORY.

In the beginning, God created the heavens and the earth.

He said, "Let there be light!" God saw that the light was good. Evening came, and then morning came. That was the first day of creation.

God spoke again: "Let there be an expanse between the waters to separate them." God called the expanse *sky*. Evening came, and then morning came. That was the second day of creation.

God said, "Let the water under the sky be gathered into one place, and let the dry land appear." God saw that it was good. Then God said, "Let the earth make plants and trees with fruits and seeds." Evening came, and then morning came. That was the third day of creation.

Next, God placed lights in the sky. God created the sun to shine during the day and the moon and stars to shine at night. God saw that it was good. Evening came, and then morning came. That was the fourth day of creation.

Next, God made creatures that move and swim in the water. God saw that it was good. Evening came, and then morning came. That was the fifth day of creation.

Then God made more animals, and God saw that it was good.

Christ Connection: The Bible says that Jesus is Lord over all of creation. Everything was created by Him and for Him. The Son has always existed, and He holds everything together. (Colossians 1:16-17)

God Created People
Genesis 1:26–2:25

MAIN POINT: GOD CREATED PEOPLE IN HIS OWN IMAGE; GOD CREATED THEM MALE AND FEMALE.

On the sixth day of creation, God made people in His very own image. God took dust from the ground and made a man. God told the man to work in the garden and take care of it.

God provided food from the trees for the man to eat. Then God said, "You can eat from any of the trees in the garden, except for one." God warned the man, "If you eat from that tree, you will die."

God decided to make a helper for the man. God made wild animals and birds, but none of the animals was a good helper for the man.

So God made the man fall fast asleep. He took one of the man's ribs and created a woman.

The woman was a perfect helper for the man. The man's name was Adam, and his wife's name was Eve.

God looked at everything He had made, and it was very good. On the seventh day of creation, God rested.

Christ Connection: God created people in His own image. Adam was like God in some ways, but he was not a perfect representation of God. God sent His Son, Jesus, to show us exactly what God is like. (Colossians 1:15) Jesus is the perfect representation of God because He is God. (Hebrews 1:3)

Sin Entered the World
Genesis 3:1-24

MAIN POINT: ADAM AND EVE'S SIN SEPARATED THEM FROM GOD.

God gave Adam and Eve a beautiful garden to live in. God also gave them one command. He told Adam that he could eat from any tree in the garden except for one. God said that if Adam did eat from the tree, he would die.

Now the serpent was the most cunning of all the animals. One day, the serpent asked Eve, "Did God really say, 'You can't eat from any tree in the garden'?"

Eve answered, "God told us not to eat from the tree in the middle of the garden. If we eat the fruit or touch it, we will die."

"You will not die," the serpent said. The serpent told Eve that rather than dying, she and Adam would be like God!

Eve took some of the fruit and ate it. Eve also gave some of the fruit to Adam, who was with her, and he ate it.

Then their eyes were opened, and they knew they were naked.

That evening, Adam and Eve heard God walking in the garden. They hid among the trees. God called out to Adam, "Where are you?"

God asked, "Did you eat from the tree I commanded you not to eat from?"

Adam blamed Eve. Eve blamed the serpent.

God said that because of the serpent's trick and Adam and Eve's disobedience, bad things would happen. But God promised that one of Eve's descendants would destroy the serpent.

Everything changed after Adam and Eve sinned. Sin separated Adam and Eve from God. God sent them out of the garden. God put an angel at the entrance of the garden to guard the way to the tree of life.

Christ Connection: Since Adam and Eve, everyone has sinned against God. Our sin separates us from God. God promised that one of Eve's descendants would put an end to sin and death. God sent His Son, Jesus, to live as Adam didn't—perfectly sinless. God the Son came into the world to rescue people from sin and bring them back to God.

Cain and Abel
Genesis 4:1-16,25-26

MAIN POINT: CAIN'S SIN SEPARATED HIM FROM GOD AND PEOPLE.

Adam and Eve had a son named Cain and another son named Abel. Abel became a shepherd, and Cain worked the ground.

One day, Cain gave God an offering of the produce he grew. Abel gave God some of the firstborn of his flock. God accepted Abel's offering, but He did not accept Cain's offering.

Cain was furious. God warned Cain that sin was crouching at the door, waiting to control Cain if he did not do what is right.

Then Cain invited Abel to go out into the field. While they were in the field, Cain killed his brother.

God knew what had happened. He said to Cain, "What have you done?"

God punished Cain. God told Cain that he would spend the rest of his life wandering the earth. If Cain tried to work the ground, nothing would grow for him.

"This punishment is too much!" Cain said.

Cain left the land and went to live in Nod.

God gave Adam and Eve another son. They named him Seth. Around this time, people began to call on the name of the Lord.

Christ Connection: God had promised that one of Eve's descendants would put an end to sin and death. Cain was not that descendant. He was sinful like his parents, Adam and Eve. So people kept living and trusting God to keep His promise. At just the right time, God would send His Son to save sinners. (Hebrews 11:13; Galatians 4:4)

Noah and the Ark
Genesis 6:5–9:17

MAIN POINT: GOD IS HOLY, AND HE PUNISHES SIN.

One day God looked at all the people on earth and saw that they were choosing to sin. God was sad that He made people. God had to punish the people for their sin.

But God graciously decided to save one man: Noah. Noah followed God. God told Noah to make an ark to save himself, his family, and some of the animals. God told Noah exactly how to make the ark. Noah did everything that God commanded him.

When the ark was finished, God told Noah to go inside with his family and the animals. God said that rain was coming, and the rain would not stop for 40 days and 40 nights. Noah did what God said.

The floodwaters covered the earth, and the ark floated on top of the water. The water rose higher and higher until all of the mountains were covered. Every living thing on the earth died; only Noah and those that were with him survived.

Finally, the rain stopped and the water started to go down. When the ground was dry, God told Noah to bring all the people and animals out of the ark. He promised Noah that He would never completely flood the earth again.

God told Noah and his family to spread out over the earth and fill it with people. God placed a rainbow in the sky so that every time Noah and his family saw the rainbow, they would know God remembered the promise He made with all the living creatures on earth.

Christ Connection: God rescued Noah and his family from the flood; only they lived. The story of Noah points ahead to a greater rescue. God's Son, Jesus—the only perfectly righteous One—came to take the punishment for our sin. By trusting in Him, we are saved from the punishment our sin deserves. Jesus died so that we can live.

The Tower of Babel
Genesis 11:1-9

MAIN POINT: GOD CREATED PEOPLE TO GIVE GLORY TO HIM ALONE.

After the great flood, God told Noah and his sons to grow their families and fill the earth. Noah's sons got married and had children, and the people started to travel through the land.

At this time, everyone in the world spoke the same language. One day, the people traveled through a valley, and they decided to live there.

"We don't want to be scattered all over the earth," they said. "Let's build a city and a tower so big that it touches the sky. The tower will make us famous!"

The people were not doing what God had told them to do. They were saying "Look how great we are," instead of "Look how great God is." But God is greater than anyone. God created people to give glory to Him alone.

The people used stones to start building the tower. God came down to look at the tower. God said, "They will keep thinking up more bad things to do. We need to stop them."

So God mixed up the people's words. When people tried to make plans, they could not understand what other people were saying.

The people had to stop building the city. Families had to move away from each other to live with people they could understand. The city with the unfinished tower was called Babel. Because the people chose to disobey God, their sin separated them from one another.

Christ Connection: People chose to give glory to themselves instead of God. They ignored God's plan, so God confused their language and scattered the people all over the earth. One day, Jesus will gather together all of God's people—people from every tribe and people who speak all kinds of languages—and they will worship Him. (Revelation 7:9-10)

God's Covenant with Abraham
Genesis 12:1-3; 15:1-21; 17:1-9

MAIN POINT: GOD PROMISED TO BLESS ALL THE WORLD THROUGH ABRAHAM.

God chose Abram and told him to move to a place he had never been. God promised Abram three things: a large family, land for his family, and blessing.

This was a good promise, but Abram was sad. He didn't have any children to inherit his blessing. God took Abram outside to remind him of His promise. "Look at the sky and count the stars, if you can," God said. "Your family will be that numerous." Abram believed God, and God was pleased.

God also promised that Abram's family would keep the land they were in. Abram asked, "How can I be sure?" So God confirmed His covenant with Abram.

God told Abram to bring five animals: a cow, a goat, a ram, a turtledove, and a pigeon. Abram did as God said, and he divided the animals. Then, when the sun was setting, a deep sleep came over him.

While Abram slept, God told him what would happen in the future. When it was dark, a smoking fire pot and a flaming torch representing God passed between the animals. This showed that God would be responsible for keeping His promise.

Many years passed and Abram still didn't have the promised son. God hadn't forgotten, though. He reminded Abram, "I am God Almighty. I will establish My covenant between Me and you, and I will multiply you greatly."

God was so serious about His promise that He changed Abram's name to Abraham, which means "Father of a Great Multitude."

"I will keep My promise to you, God said, "and it will last forever. I will be your God, and I will be the God of your family—of all your descendants."

Christ Connection: God called Abraham to leave his country and family to go to another land. God promised to bless all the world through Abraham. God sent Jesus from His home in heaven to be born on earth into Abraham's family. Through Jesus, all the nations of the earth are blessed.

God Tested Abraham
Genesis 22:1-19

MAIN POINT: ABRAHAM TRUSTED GOD EVEN WHEN HE DIDN'T UNDERSTAND GOD'S PLAN.

God kept His promise to give Abraham a son. Abraham and his wife Sarah were very old when their son Isaac was born. One day, God tested Abraham. God wanted to make sure that Abraham loved God most of all.

"Take your son Isaac to the mountain and give him to Me as a sacrifice," God said. Abraham obeyed God. He got up early the next day and left with Isaac, two servants, and a donkey carrying supplies. They walked for three days before they got to the mountain where God wanted Abraham to make the sacrifice. Abraham and Isaac went up the mountain with the supplies for the sacrifice.

Isaac noticed something was missing. "My father," he said, "where is the lamb for the offering?"

Abraham answered, "God Himself will provide the lamb."

When they got to the place God had directed them, Abraham built an altar and placed the wood on top. Then he put Isaac on top of the wood. Just as Abraham was about to sacrifice Isaac, the Angel of the Lord called out, "Abraham, Abraham!"

Abraham stopped. The Angel of the Lord said, "Do not lay a hand on the boy or do anything to him. For now I know that you fear God, since you have not withheld your only son from Me."

Abraham looked up and saw a ram trapped by its horns in the bushes. He offered to God the ram instead of Isaac.

Christ Connection: Abraham showed his love for God by being willing to sacrifice his son Isaac. This is how God showed His love for us: He sent His Son, Jesus, to die on the cross so that we could have eternal life through Him.

The Promise Reaffirmed
Genesis 25:19-26; 26:1-6; 28:10-22

MAIN POINT: GOD REMINDED ABRAHAM'S FAMILY THAT HE ALWAYS KEEPS HIS PROMISES.

Abraham's son Isaac grew up and married a woman named Rebekah. For many years, Isaac and Rebekah did not have any children, so Isaac prayed and asked God for a child. God answered Isaac's prayer, and Rebekah became pregnant with twins. The two babies fought inside of Rebekah, and she was worried.

"Why is this happening?" Rebekah asked the Lord. The Lord told Rebekah part of His special plan. When Rebekah's babies were born, the first brother was named Esau (EE saw). The younger brother was named Jacob.

Later, God appeared to Isaac to give him a special message about His plan for Isaac and his family. God shared with Isaac the special covenant He had made with Isaac's father, Abraham. God said, "I will give all these lands to you and your family. I will make your family as numerous as the stars of the sky. All the nations of the earth will be blessed by your family because Abraham, your father, listened to My voice and obeyed My words."

Many years later, Isaac's sons Jacob and Esau fought. Jacob tricked Isaac and stole Esau's blessing. Jacob had to leave his family to stay safe. On his way to his uncle's house, Jacob stopped at night to sleep.

While Jacob slept, he had a dream. In his dream, Jacob saw a stairway coming down from heaven to the ground. Angels were going up and down the stairs.

Then Jacob saw God, and God spoke to him. God promised to be with Jacob. "I am with you and will watch over you wherever you go," He said.

Jacob woke up and said, "Surely the Lord is in this place. What an awesome place this is."

Christ Connection: God's wonderful plan to Abraham extended well beyond his lifetime. The plan was shared with Rebekah, Isaac, Jacob, and eventually an entire nation leading to the birth of a baby boy named Jesus. Jesus fulfilled God's plan to provide salvation and redemption for all of God's people.

The Stolen Blessing
Genesis 25:27-34; 27:1-45

MAIN POINT: JACOB STOLE ESAU'S BLESSING.

Jacob and Esau were brothers. Esau was a hunter while Jacob worked at home. One day, Jacob was cooking lentil stew when his brother came home from the field. "I am exhausted!" he said. "Let me eat some of that red stuff."

Jacob answered, "First sell me your birthright." Whoever had the birthright got more of his family's belongings when his parents died.

"I'm so hungry, I'm about to die!" Esau replied. He agreed to give Jacob his birthright for stew and bread.

Now their father Isaac was getting old and losing his eyesight. Isaac called for Esau. "I want to bless you before I die," Isaac said. Isaac asked Esau to bring back food from a hunt and cook it for him.

Rebekah heard Isaac and Esau talking. She told her son Jacob what was happening and came up with her own plan. Rebecca made Isaac's favorite meal. She put Esau's clothes on Jacob and covered his skin with goat hair so that Isaac would think Jacob was Esau. Then Jacob took the meal to his father.

"Who are you, my son?" Isaac asked.

"I am Esau, your firstborn. I have done as you told me," Jacob said.

After the meal, Isaac offered him the blessing. The blessing included land, riches, and power. Then Jacob left.

About this time, Esau came home and cooked a meal for his father. When he offered the food to Isaac, his father told him that he had been tricked. Esau cried and begged his father to bless him, too. But Isaac had nothing left to offer Esau. Esau was angry at his brother Jacob, and he made a plan to kill him. But Rebekah sent Jacob away.

Christ Connection: Jesus is the firstborn over all creation. (Colossians 1:15) When Jesus hung on the cross, He gave up His blessing for us. Jesus took the punishment we deserve so that the Father would give us the blessing He deserves.

Jacob's New Name
Genesis 32–33

MAIN POINT: GOD CHANGED JACOB'S NAME TO ISRAEL, THE NAME OF GOD'S COVENANT PEOPLE.

God had made a covenant with Jacob's grandfather Abraham. Then God told His promise to Jacob's father, Isaac. God had a plan for Jacob too.

Years before, Jacob tricked his father and his brother; he stole the blessing from Esau. Then Jacob ran away to escape Esau's anger. God met with Jacob and promised to be with him. Now God told Jacob that it was time to go home.

Jacob was afraid that Esau would still be angry with him for stealing his blessing. Jacob made a plan. He divided his family into two groups. If Esau attacked one group, maybe the other group could escape. Then Jacob prayed. He asked God to keep His promise. Jacob sent a large gift of animals to try to make Esau happy.

That night, a man appeared. (The man was actually God Himself!) The man wrestled with Jacob all night. Jacob refused to give up, so the man injured Jacob's hip. But Jacob would not let Him go. "I will not let You go unless You bless me," Jacob said.

"Your name will no longer be Jacob," said the man. "Your name will be Israel because you wrestled with God and with men, and you have won." The man blessed Jacob.

Now Jacob went to meet Esau. Esau ran to Jacob and hugged him. He was not angry anymore. Jacob bought land for his family to live on. He was finally home in the land God had promised him.

Christ Connection: God changed Jacob's life and gave him a new name, Israel. Jesus came so that we might have a changed life, forgiven of sin. (2 Corinthians 5:17) Jesus' death and resurrection provided sinful people with the way to be adopted into God's family. When we are adopted into the family of God we also receive a new name—children of God. (John 1:12)

Joseph Sent to Egypt
Genesis 37:1-36; 39:1–41:57

MAIN POINT: GOD USED JOSEPH'S SUFFERING FOR GOOD.

Jacob had 12 sons, but his favorite son was Joseph. Jacob gave Joseph a colorful robe. The other brothers saw that their father loved Joseph the most, and they hated Joseph.

One day, Jacob sent Joseph to check on his brothers, who were tending to the family's sheep. When the brothers saw him coming, they decided to kill him. Joseph's oldest brother convinced the others to throw him into a pit instead.

The brothers saw a caravan of people heading to Egypt, and they sold Joseph to them as a servant.

The travelers sold Joseph to an Egyptian officer named Potiphar. But Potiphar's wife accused Joseph of doing something he didn't do. Potiphar believed his wife, and Joseph was thrown into jail.

Even in jail, God was with Joseph. The jail warden put Joseph in charge of the other prisoners. Joseph cared for two of Pharaoh's top officials. Joseph told them what the dreams meant. Joseph said that one day, the cupbearer would serve Pharaoh again. Joseph asked the cupbearer to remember him and to tell Pharaoh that he did not deserve to be in jail.

Pharaoh had two dreams. Pharaoh saw seven fat cows eaten by seven skinny cows, and seven fat heads of grain eaten by seven thin heads. No one knew what these dreams meant! That's when the cupbearer remembered Joseph. God told Joseph what Pharaoh's dreams meant, and Joseph explained the dreams to Pharaoh. Then Pharaoh made Joseph second in command in all of Egypt.

Joseph stored away food during the good years, and during the famine, people came from all nations to buy grain from Joseph.

Christ Connection: God sent Joseph to Egypt and blessed him so that he rose to a position of great power. God used Joseph to save Joseph's family and many others from death by starvation. Jesus gave up his position of great power to be the Savior of the world.

Joseph's Dreams Came True
Genesis 42:1–46:34; 50:15-21

MAIN POINT: GOD SENT JOSEPH TO EGYPT TO ESTABLISH A REMNANT.

Jacob and his family did not have enough food to eat. But Jacob learned that there was food in Egypt. So Jacob sent 10 of his sons to buy some grain. His youngest son, Benjamin, stayed home.

Joseph was in charge of who got food, so the brothers came to him and bowed down. Joseph knew who these men were, but they did not recognize him.

Joseph said, "I think you are spies. You are here to spy on the land."

Then he said, "Go home and bring your youngest brother back to me to prove that you are not spies. But one of you must stay here."

The brothers went home with food for their families, and one of them stayed in Egypt. They told their father everything that had happened, and their father was very upset. "Do not take my youngest son with you," he said. "Joseph is dead, and I cannot lose another son."

But when all the food was gone, Jacob asked his sons to go back to Egypt. Benjamin went too. Joseph invited all of the brothers to his home for a meal. "I am Joseph!" he told them. "You sold me into Egypt, but do not be afraid. God sent me here so I could save your people, a remnant, from the famine."

Joseph told his brothers to go home and gather all their family and belongings and come back to Egypt, where they would have enough food to eat.

Jacob's family was blessed in Egypt, but Jacob got older and died. Now Joseph's brothers were afraid Joseph would punish them for what they did to him. Joseph said, "You planned evil against me; God planned it for good."

Christ Connection: God had a plan for Joseph's life. He allowed Joseph to suffer in order to rescue a whole nation. God planned for Jesus to suffer so that many—people from all nations—would be saved.

Moses Was Born and Called
Exodus 1:8–2:10,23-25; 3:1–4:20

MAIN POINT: GOD RESCUED MOSES TO DELIVER HIS PEOPLE FROM CAPTIVITY.

Years after Joseph brought his family to Egypt, Joseph died. His family stayed in Egypt. The people in the family were known as Israelites.

A new pharaoh came to power, and he was afraid of the Israelites. Pharaoh made them slaves and gave them very hard work to do, but their families kept growing!

"Kill all the baby boys!" Pharaoh said.

Around this time, a Hebrew woman gave birth to a son. She hid him as long as she could, and then she put him in a basket and set it along the banks of the Nile. The baby's older sister, Miriam, stayed nearby and watched the basket.

Pharaoh's daughter found the basket and felt sorry for the baby. She wanted him to be her son. The princess named the baby Moses.

When Moses grew up, he had to leave Egypt. The Israelite people cried out to God. God heard them, and He planned to send Moses to help them.

One day, Moses saw a burning bush. Suddenly, God called from the bush, "Moses, Moses!"

Moses replied, "Here I am."

God said, "I have seen how My people are suffering. I want you to lead them out of Egypt to a good land I have for them."

"What if they ask for Your name? What should I tell them?"

"I AM WHO I AM," God said.

Moses made excuses and said, "Please send someone else." Now God was angry, but He agreed to send Moses' brother, Aaron, with him.

Christ Connection: God saved Moses to rescue His people. The calling of Moses points to a greater calling and rescue—the call of Jesus to come to earth to save God's people from sin. Moses and Jesus both obeyed God's commands in order to carry out His plan of salvation. Moses delivered God's people from physical captivity; Jesus delivered God's people from captivity to sin.

The Plagues, the Passover, and the Crossing of the Red Sea

Exodus 5–14

MAIN POINT: GOD PROVED TO THE EGYPTIANS THAT HE IS THE ONE TRUE GOD.

The Israelites were slaves in Egypt. God planned to use Moses to rescue them. So Moses and his brother told Pharaoh, "Let My people go." Pharaoh responded, "Israel may not go!" So God sent a set of plagues to punish the Egyptians.

God turned the water in the Nile River into blood and sent frogs into Egypt. Pharaoh refused to let the people go. God sent gnats and flies. But Pharaoh did not let the people go. God caused all the livestock to die, and He sent boils. But Pharaoh's heart was hard. God sent a terrible hailstorm to Egypt. He sent locusts.

Pharaoh refused to let the Israelites go. So God sent darkness to cover the land. But Pharaoh said no. Moses warned Pharaoh. God would go through Egypt. Every firstborn male would die, but the Israelites would be safe. Pharaoh ignored Moses.

God told every Israelite family to kill a lamb and sprinkle its blood on the doorposts of their houses. This would be a special mark that God would see and "pass over." No one in the Israelites' families would die.

At midnight, God struck every firstborn in the land of Egypt. Pharaoh called for Moses and Aaron. "Go!" he said. The Israelites quickly left Egypt.

Pharaoh and his officials came after the Israelites and caught up with them near the sea. God told Moses to stretch out his hand and divide the sea so that the Israelites could go through on dry ground. The Israelites walked through with walls of water on both sides. Moses stretched out his hand again and the waters returned. None of Pharaoh's army survived.

Christ Connection: At Passover, God spared the Israelites from judgment by requiring the blood of a lamb. Moses led the Israelites out of Egypt, and God provided a way for them to escape through the Red Sea. The Bible says that Jesus is greater than Moses. (Hebrews 3:3) Jesus is the Lamb of God, who takes away the sin of the world. People who trust in Jesus escape the penalty of sin and have eternal life.

The Wilderness Test

Exodus 15:22–17:7

MAIN POINT: GOD PROVIDED FOR THE PHYSICAL NEEDS OF HIS PEOPLE.

Moses led the people to the wilderness. They could not find good water to drink, and they complained to Moses. God said, "If you obey Me and do what is right and keep My commands, I will not punish you like I punished the Egyptians."

The Israelites journeyed into the wilderness. They were hungry and they complained to Moses.

God said, "I have heard the complaints of the Israelites. Tell them: In the evening you will eat meat, and in the morning you will eat bread until you are full. Then you will know that I am Yahweh your God."

So at evening, quail came into the camp. In the morning, fine flakes like frost were on the ground.

God told them to collect just enough to eat for the day. If they collected too much, the leftovers went bad. He told them to collect twice as much on the sixth day, because the seventh day was the Sabbath, a day to rest. The Israelites ate manna for 40 years while they were in the wilderness.

The Israelites moved about the wilderness as the Lord told them to do. One day, they came to a camp with no water. "Give us something to drink," they told Moses.

"Lord, what should I do?" Moses cried out. God showed Moses a rock and instructed him to hit it with his staff. Water came out of it, and the people drank. It was a sign that the Lord was with them.

Christ Connection: In the New Testament, Jesus said that He is the Bread of life. (John 6:31-35) God provided manna from heaven for His people's physical hunger, and later He provided His Son, Jesus, for our spiritual hunger. The Israelites needed bread to live for a little while, but whoever has Jesus will live forever!

The Golden Calf
Exodus 32:1–35; 34:1–9

MAIN POINT: GOD PUNISHED HIS PEOPLE FOR WORSHIPING A GOLDEN CALF.

Moses and the Israelites came to Mount Sinai. Moses went up the mountain, and God spoke to him. Moses was up on Mount Sinai for 40 days and 40 nights. Meanwhile, the Israelites camping at the base of the mountain were getting impatient. They went to Moses' brother, Aaron. "Make us a god to lead us," they said. So Aaron made a gold calf that they could worship.

God saw what the people were doing, and He was angry because of their sin. "Please forgive them," Moses said. "Remember the great promise You made to Abraham, Isaac, and Jacob." So God decided not to destroy them.

Moses went down the mountain. He carried two stone tablets on which God had written the laws. Moses got closer to the camp and saw that the people were dancing before the gold calf! He threw down the stone tablets, smashing them at the bottom of the mountain. Then he destroyed the calf they made.

The next day, Moses said, "I will go up to the Lord. Maybe I can do something to make up for your sin."

Moses said to God, "Please forgive their sin."

God continued to meet with Moses and give him laws and instructions. He made two more stone tablets to replace the ones Moses broke. One morning, Moses went up the mountain to meet with God. The Lord said, "Yahweh is a compassionate and gracious God ... but He will not leave the guilty unpunished."

Moses bowed down and worshiped God. "Lord, please go with us," he said. "Forgive our sin, and accept us as Your people."

Christ Connection: God's people sinned against God, and Moses asked God to forgive them. Moses acted as their mediator, standing for them before God. Moses could not do anything to make up for their sin, but we have a better Mediator—Jesus. Jesus paid for our sin on the cross and stands for us before God. When we trust in Jesus, our sins are forgiven.

The Ten Commandments: Love God
Exodus 19:1–20:11; 31:18

MAIN POINT: GOD GAVE US RULES TO SHOW THAT HE IS HOLY AND WE ARE SINNERS.

Three months after the Israelites left Egypt, they came into the Wilderness of Sinai. They camped in front of the mountain.

Moses went up the mountain. God called to him, saying, "This is what you should tell the Israelites: 'If you listen carefully to Me and you keep My covenant, you will be My people.'"

Moses went back to the people and told them what God had said. All the people agreed.

The Lord said to Moses, "I am going to come to you in a dense cloud. I want the people to hear Me speak to you so that they will believe you."

Moses got the people ready for the Lord to come down on the mountain.

On the morning of the third day, thunder rumbled and lightning lit up the sky. A thick cloud came down on the mountain, and a loud trumpet sounded. Moses brought the people out of the camp to meet God, and they stood at the foot of the mountain.

God came down on Mount Sinai in a fire, and smoke covered the mountain. "I am the Lord your God, who brought you out of the land of Egypt. I freed you from slavery," He said.

Then God gave Moses the Ten Commandments. These are the first four commandments. These commandments told the Israelites what it looks like to have a right relationship with God: "Do not have other gods besides Me. Do not make an idol for yourself. Do not misuse the name of the Lord your God. Remember the Sabbath day, to keep it holy."

Christ Connection: God is holy and separate from sin. His law shows us what He requires—perfect righteousness. Our sin separates us from God, but Jesus came to bring us back to God. Jesus is perfectly righteous. When we trust in Jesus, He takes away our sin and welcomes us into God's family.

The Ten Commandments: Love Others

Exodus 20:12-17

MAIN POINT: GOD GAVE US RULES TO HELP US KNOW HOW TO LOVE HIM AND OTHERS.

Moses and the Israelites were in the wilderness, camped at the base of Mount Sinai. God made a covenant, or agreement, with the people of Israel.

God said, "If you listen carefully to Me and keep My covenant, you will be My people."

The Israelites agreed to do everything the Lord said.

Moses went up the mountain, and the Lord came down in a fire.

God gave Moses the Ten Commandments. The last six commandments told the Israelites what it looks like to have a right relationship with each other: " … You must honor your father and your mother. You must not murder. You must keep your marriage promises. You must not steal. You must not lie. You must not want what belongs to someone else."

Moses was on the mountain for 40 days. God gave Moses many more laws. When God was finished speaking to Moses on Mount Sinai, He gave Moses two stone tablets that He had written on with His own finger.

Christ Connection: God's law shows us what He requires—perfect righteousness. Everyone has sinned against God and against each other. God sent His Son, Jesus, to live the perfect life we have not lived and to take the punishment we deserve for our sin. When we trust in Jesus, God forgives our sin and gives us eternal life.

The Tabernacle Was Built

Exodus 35:4–40:38

MAIN POINT: GOD TOLD HIS PEOPLE TO BUILD THE TABERNACLE SO HE COULD DWELL WITH THEM.

When Moses was on the mountain with God, God said, "Tell the Israelites to make a tabernacle for Me so that I may dwell among them."

"Make it exactly like I show you," God said. The tabernacle would be where God met with His people.

So when Moses went down the mountain, he gathered the entire Israelite community together. He told them everything God had said. Every Israelite who wanted to brought materials as an offering for the tabernacle.

Pretty soon, the craftsmen came to Moses and said, "The people are bringing more than enough. We don't need all of this." So Moses told the Israelites to stop bringing their offerings.

They built the tabernacle just as God had instructed. When the time came, God told Moses how to set up the tabernacle. God told him how to anoint the tabernacle so that it would be holy.

God told Moses to bring Aaron and his sons to the entrance of the tabernacle. Aaron put on the holy garments and Moses anointed him to be priest. Aaron's sons were also anointed to serve God as priests. Moses did exactly what God commanded, and the tabernacle was finally finished.

God had led the Israelites from a cloud, and now the cloud covered the tabernacle. God's glory filled the tabernacle.

Christ Connection: God instructed the Israelites to build a tabernacle so that He could dwell with them. God desires to be with His people. As part of His plan of salvation, God sent Jesus to "tabernacle," or dwell with people on earth.

God Gave Rules for Sacrifice
Leviticus 1–27

MAIN POINT: BECAUSE GOD IS HOLY, GOD REQUIRES A SACRIFICE FOR SIN.

When Moses was with God on Mount Sinai, God gave him many laws. He gave the people rules about how to live, how to worship God, and what to do when they sinned.

First, God gave rules about offerings. Offerings are gifts people give to God. Different types of offerings were needed at different times. When people wanted to praise God, they gave burnt offerings. When they wanted to say they were sorry for sin, they gave a sin offering.

God also gave rules about the priests. Priests made the sacrifices that God commanded. The priests took care of the tabernacle, and they taught the people God's rules for living holy lives.

God told Moses about a special day that would happen once a year. It was called the Day of Atonement. On the Day of Atonement, the people paid for their sins. The high priest offered a special sacrifice.

The sacrifice was important because it paid for the sins of the people of Israel.

God also gave the Israelites rules about how they should live. He said, "Be holy because I, Yahweh your God, am holy."

Christ Connection: The sacrifices God required of His people were a hint of what God was going to do to forgive sinners. We no longer need to offer sacrifices because we trust in Jesus. Jesus offered Himself as the perfect sacrifice that takes away our sin once and for all.

Worship Only God
Deuteronomy 1; 3:23–4:40

MAIN POINT: THE LORD ALONE IS GOD; THERE IS NO OTHER BESIDES HIM.

Moses and the Israelites had wandered in the wilderness for 40 years. Now the Israelites were at the edge of the promised land—the land God had promised to give to His people. But before they entered the land, Moses told the Israelites everything God had commanded him to say.

First, Moses reminded the people of why they were in the wilderness. "Many years ago, God told us to enter the promised land," Moses said. "But the people refused to go in. They were afraid of the people who lived there."

So God said that everyone who chose to disobey Him would not enter the promised land—not even me. Only their children and Joshua and Caleb (who had trusted God completely) would go in.

"Now it is time for God's people to enter the promised land," he said.

Since Moses was old, he wanted to remind the Israelites of God's commands.

"Follow these commands when you live in the promised land," Moses said. "Don't forget them, and don't forget what the Lord has done. Teach these things to your children and grandchildren."

Moses told the people to remember all the things God had done. Moses said, "Know this: The Lord alone is God; there is no other besides Him."

Moses said it again. "The Lord alone is God; there is no other besides Him. Obey His commands so that you may live long in the land the Lord is giving you."

Christ Connection: Moses commanded the people to obey God so that they would live. He told them to worship only God—the one true God. We receive eternal life from God by trusting in His Son, Jesus, and we obey Him because only He is God.

God Reminded His People of His Covenant

Deuteronomy 5:1-6:25; 8:1-11:1,26-28

MAIN POINT: GOD REMINDED HIS PEOPLE OF HIS COVENANT WITH THEM.

God had an important message for the Israelites, and He spoke through Moses. "Here are the rules and laws I am telling you today. Learn them and obey them," Moses said.

Moses reminded the people that God had made a covenant, or agreement, with the Israelites at Mount Sinai. God said, "If you listen carefully to Me and keep My covenant, you will be My people."

God gave them the Ten Commandments.

"God wants you to obey all of His commands," Moses said. "God wants me to teach you all of His rules and laws, and He wants you to obey them exactly as He commanded. If you do, things will go well in the land He promised to give you, and you will live there for a long time.

"Israel, listen to me! The Lord our God, the Lord is One. Love the Lord your God with all your heart, with all your soul, and with all your strength.

"When you get to the promised land, don't forget the Lord. Remember what He has done for you. The Lord rescued you from slavery in Egypt. Worship Him, and worship only Him."

Then Moses made a very important point. "God is not doing this because you are righteous," he said. "God is keeping the promise He made to Abraham, Isaac, and Jacob."

Finally, Moses said, "Love the Lord your God. If you obey His commands, you will be blessed. If you do not obey, you will be punished."

Christ Connection: God kept His promise to give land to the families of Abraham, Isaac, and Jacob. As the Israelites stood at the edge of the promised land, God reminded them of His covenant. He commanded them to be holy and to obey Him, but He knew they would not. God was working out His plan to send Jesus to rescue people from sin and bless the whole earth.

DID YOU KNOW?

There are 5 more semesters of TGP Home Edition that will take you through the whole story of the Bible – and how every story points to Jesus!

Each of the Bible stories and teaching pictures on pages 50-61 correspond with the Bible story videos on the DVD. There are 23 in all, so some weeks you will have more than one Bible story and video. Follow the instructions for how to use them in *The Gospel Project: Home Edition Teacher's Guide Semester 1.*

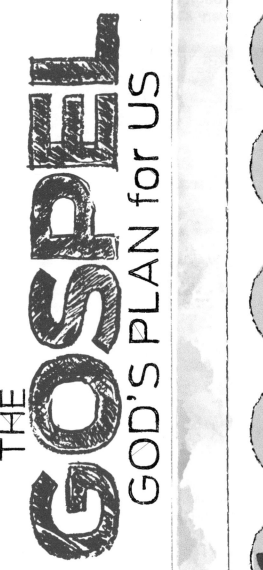

The gospel is the good news, the message about Christ, the kingdom of God, and salvation. Use these prompts to share the gospel with your kids.

GOD RULES. Ask: "Who is in charge at home?" Explain that because God created everything, He is in charge of everything. Read Revelation 4:11.

WE SINNED. Ask: "Have you ever done something wrong?" Tell kids that everyone sins, or disobeys God. Our sin separates us from God. Read Romans 3:23.

GOD PROVIDED. Explain that God is holy and must punish sin. God sent His Son, Jesus, to take the punishment we deserve. Read John 3:16.

JESUS GIVES. Ask: "What is the best gift you've ever received?" Say that Jesus took our punishment for sin by giving His life, and He gives us His righteousness. God sees us as if we lived the perfect life Jesus lived. This is the best gift ever! Read 2 Corinthians 5:21.

WE RESPOND. Explain that everyone has a choice to make. Ask: "Will you trust Jesus as your Savior and Lord? You can turn from self and sin and turn to Jesus." Read Romans 10:9-10.